A Rare Class

Living A Lifestyle You Can Be Proud To Call Your Own

Leandrea Rivers

Library of Congress Cataloging-in-Publication Data

© 2021 by Leandrea Rivers

All rights reserved. No part of this publication may be reproduced, stored, or transmitted in any form or by any means, electronic, mechanical, photocopying, recording, scanning, or otherwise without written permission from the publisher. It is illegal to copy this book, post it to a website, or distribute it by any other means without permission.

Scriptures are taken from the KING JAMES VERSION (KJV):

KING JAMES VERSION, public domain.

First edition

ISBN: 978-0-9964713-2-9

Cover Design by Barbara Upshaw-Mayers

Editing by Paula McDade

Interior Formatting & Layout, by Jamarr Williams

Back cover photograph: Tierra Michel

Dedication

Living a lifestyle that I can be proud to call my own no longer became my own lifestyle the moment my three beautiful grandchildren were born. Through them I now understand the word agape – unconditional love; how God loves us. The ability to love through it all, without conditions. It is simply pure love at its rarest form.

It became clear incredibly early on when our eyes met, and our hearts touched a need for an established legacy. It would no longer be enough to simply impart into them principles and my pearls of wisdom alone. No, I wanted to ensure they have opportunities that was not afforded to their dad, my son.

Each generation should be greater than the one which precedes them... It is my hope, my prayer, my wish for you my beautiful grands; that you far exceed any generation before you. All my love, all my gifts and all my talents I pour into your future. May your future forever reign BRIGHT my loves...

-GiGi

Preface

If you are looking for a book to teach you how to "fake it until you make it" please close now, this is not the one for you! However, if you want to enjoy a lifestyle appreciating life's absolute best… You have found your book.

In "A Rare Class" I look forward to sharing the beauty of living a simplistic lifestyle by decluttering your mind, home life and relation-ships by improving your perceptions on how you view your lifestyle and those around you. I will help you to take a closer look at the things surrounding your everyday life; behaviors, attitudes and the tangible things that no longer have value opposed to those that do! As a bonus, I will share shopping secrets for home décor, fashion, quality "must haves" verses quantity, luxury discounts and removing the chaos from your life through practical organizational skills.

This book was written with every intent to share secrets to living a lifestyle you can be proud to call your own. It is with my deepest pleasure to help you as an individual understand your perception of your current lifestyle and the way you view the lifestyle of those around you. "A Rare Class" is designed to help remove the social stigma which prevents many from achieving their goals and instead embrace a new way of living the lifestyle you have always imagined.

Whatever lifestyle you choose, only you can define your happiness "be proud to call your lifestyle your own!"

Living A Lifestyle You Can Be Proud To Call Your Own

Contents

	Dedication	v
	Preface	vii
1	Secret Workshop	12
2	Perfect Lifestyle	18
3	Luxury Isn't For The Faint At Heart	24
4	Simplicities	31
5	The "A" List	40
6	Are We Clear To Enter?	46
7	The Exclusive Club	52
8	A Diamond In The Rough	56
9	The Elite Class	60
10	Shower Me	64
11	Who's The Boss	68
12	Friend of Foe	73
13	Unbothered	77
14	Worthy	81
15	Don't Speak	85
16	Open Invitation	89
17	Shine Bright	94
18	Sharing Is Caring	98
	Closing Thoughts	101

1

Secret Workshop

How many of you have read, "idle hands are the devil's workshop?" (Proverbs 16:27-29). Many days and nights throughout my childhood left plenty of idle time. My imagination was massive and my creativity even greater. In fact, my mind was on alert 24/7.

Secretly, my entire life I battled with my identity. I never felt that I could be the person I envisioned. Why? Because of acceptance. I always cared more about what others thought of me, what was said of me and how I made others feel. Although, being raised by parents who both instilled in me to take pride in everything I set my hands to work to my appearance - my parents encouraged me to excel and give it my all.

However, no one knew my inner struggles. Some would see me and think that I was someone who had it all, but nothing could be further from the truth. My mother cautioned me since childhood of people with envious tendencies, because I was sure to be judged by appearance first and not by my character as she had in her own life. I could never fathom such a thing until I could no longer justify odd behaviors or comments when I walked into or left a room.

Truthfully, I did most things in life because they were expected of me; expected by those whose opinions I valued most - my parents, my siblings, my mate, my friends, my family or expected in my head. Very seldom did I rock the boat and if I did, I did everything I could to minimize the impact (Truthfully, I failed at this more than once).

It had become a constant battle in my head, hence the reason why ultimately, I became a writer. I could share my deepest emotions with the pen and pad, without judgment or condemnation. Finally, I was free to be who I wanted to be if, only on paper.

And who was this woman I envisioned? She was a woman of independence; free to speak freely, free to express freely, free to not overly obsess about what others thought of her or how she has made someone else feel. This woman could wear whatever she desired, without fear that she would make someone else feel less than or uncomfortable. She was a woman who could accept a compliment without a reply that diminished the compliment just given. This lady was someone who loved herself enough to say "no" sometimes. She could step out of her comfort zone and "dance as if nobody's watching."

This woman I have always envisioned would have a voice throughout the world in a capacity that would deem her as unforgettable by her acts of kindness, humility, grace, and love for helping others. And then the question lies, how can this woman come to be unless "she herself can be proud of the life she lives," without hiding behind who she wants to be verses who she is in reality?"

I discovered if I was feeling this way most of my life, that there may be others with similar feelings. Are you who you truly are because it is someone you want to be or are you being someone because of other people's expectations of you?

Today, I can honestly say that I am a woman who strives daily to be as authentic to my true self as possible. I understand I will fail;

I will disappoint. I accept that I cannot control what others may feel or how they may react - I have finally realized that I can only control me and take full accountability for me, my words, my actions, and my decisions alone. I have grown to love the woman that looks back at me in the mirror and I encourage other women and men to also love themselves.

I am an advocate of counseling. I feel everyone should see a psychologist at least once in their lifetime. I am not embarrassed at all to say that I have been on more than one occasion for various life events that were difficult for me to recover from with my skill capacity alone. However, it was through each counselor (I went to several) that I discovered more and more about myself and how to view situations from various perspectives. You see, undoubtedly the goal is always to be a better version of me. And besides, you do not want everyone knowing all your business, do you? I sure did not. All I wanted my co-workers to see when I arrived to work was a beautiful smile. I desired to leave my home life problems at home. It was through counseling that I finally understood why I had such a heart for others and why I considered myself a little different than most. I am an empath. I feel the emotions of others happiness, sadness, and anger. If someone is happy, I am genuinely happy for them. If they are hurting, I am feeling every emotion of pain they are experiencing. I cannot shake it even if I tried. Therefore, it is so difficult for me to be surrounded by negative energy, it literally sucks the life out of me. I can sense the energy a mile away.

Positive energy is a choice that is always my preference. Although, as unrealistic as it may seem at times to others, it is still my preferred preference. Anything or anyone that prevents this, and I am searching for the nearest exit as should you. Just think how this world would be a better place if we had more of this positive thinking and energy around. Thank God for wanting to understand myself and become a better me. It was through this discovery that I learned this was one of the reasons that I was eager to call it quits in some relationships or accept the fact that it could no longer continue because I would feel too much of the other person's emotions and deemed it as not being authentic or just not something that would benefit my life in a positive way in the long run. I trusted more that God gave me this gift for me to fulfill the purpose He had called for my life.

What is it about yourself, your behaviors, or thoughts that you may benefit from seeing a counselor or doing research to learn more about yourself? How can others understand you if you do not have a clear understanding of you? Are you still at the workshop with an idle mind or have you taken the necessary measures in action to ensure your life is a life you are in acceptance of for you? Are you building and if so, what are you building? What type of person or lifestyle do you desire to live? Will you begin to roll up your sleeves and put in the work?

Use the following journal page to write your thoughts.

Journal Page

Perceptions

2

Perfect Lifestyle

We explored a little about getting to know yourself better, tools and avenues to help you get there.... Now, let us switch gears for a minute and discuss "perceptions."

Let us talk perception!

Your own perception as a matter of fact. Hmmm.... Let us start here. This should be interesting. It is a gorgeous Saturday morning, and you are out and about running errands. While at the local market you see this beautiful, all black luxury sedan.... You know, just like the one your neighbors "Mr. and Mrs. Jones" drives. You know, the same couple to you who has absolutely everything – the perfect lifestyle!

You immediately begin to feel down in your spirit thinking "how on earth will I ever elevate to achieve that level of success and more?" In your mind, their lifestyle is the epitome of success. Mr. and Mrs. Jones are seven figure income earner investors blessed to receive accolades across the globe.

All of the above is your perception of their lifestyle. Now, let us dive into a dose of reality "fact checks!" The successful, prosper because they have failed time and time again before they achieve true riches; "tried and tested." Not everyone is equipped to gain and sustain wealth, if this were true everyone would be wealthy.

Do you know for a fact that The Jones' are blessed with a clear title to their luxury car? Because if they are not, chances are their vehicle is financed and can be repossessed if they default on payments. This also applies to their home(s). If financed, do you know if their payments are current? Hypothetically, it is possible that you could be in a better financial situation than this couple. Yet here you are comparing your lifestyle to theirs - it's conceivable that The Jones' could be wishing for your lifestyle instead due to their enormous debt to income ratio.

Many are immersed in debt attempting to portray this lavish life-style that is simply not reality. How someone else is living should not penetrate your existence one bit – this is their dream! Be so focused, driven, creative, purpose driven on creating your own goals, your own lifestyle, your own happiness that you won't succumb to some people's façade or blessings.

Relationships are no different. There you are, jealous because externally Mr. and Mrs. Jones are a hot couple, fit body, and extremely attractive couple. Let me ask you, are you the fly on their wall? Were you there last night when they were arguing about Mr. Jones attraction to younger women? Or were you there the other night when Mrs. Jones was crying her eyes out because financially, she does not know how they will avoid foreclosure?

Everything is not what it appears. It is your perception. Sure, they may smile for the cameras for a social media post, but they are not forcing that on you. Take it at face value because that was a single moment in time…. It was not their everyday, 24/7 life as they are walking around the house or in their cars taking trips while on cloud 9. C'mon, you are more mature than that! You must know better; it simply is not the reality of most. Yet here you are all in your feelings when you see a photo of them come down your newsfeed. Stop it!

Couples argue, they disagree and at times they separate without anyone else knowing otherwise. Some, living double lifestyles unbeknownst to the other partner. Do not make someone else's lifestyle your own. Stop it, stop comparing the two. Single people want to be married and often, married couples wish for the days of singlehood again.

Do you see where I am going with this? Everyone wants what is perceived to be "the good life" – where everyone is happy but unknowingly, those same people are wishing they were in your shoes.

Get the right shoe size and rock your own!

The same applies with many of the social celebs; both women and men you are admiring.

There are many of you comparing your flaws against makeup air-brushed models/actors, and/or VIP cosmetic surgeons' clients world-wide. Do yourself a favor by limiting the time you devote to social media. Do not consume your life with "update statuses" and "likes" if this is what defines your life then you have a lot of reading left to do. I have a lot of respect for the celebs who invite their fans to see them without all the glam; they realize how detrimental the pressure of looks can be for someone with low self-esteem issues. No one here on earth is perfect, no one!

Daily, we decide who we will become and how we choose to live. There are several inspiring testimonials of individuals who have kept it real and shared their heart wrenching experiences of triumph through discipline of physical training and diet to achieve their bodies. If you are going to be inspired, why not follow authenticity?

Remember, the key is creating a lifestyle you can be proud to call your own… not your neighbor, not your girlfriend, not your social media associates, not anyone except you! And "believe it or not," being healthy is a lifestyle; mentally and physically. It is a commitment to work hard daily on the betterment of you.

Never envy what others have, you have no clue what Mr. and Mrs. Jones' reality truly is. Some people have literally sold their souls for gain. Do not allow others to paint a picture for you of what your desires should be. Your lifestyle is yours to choose. Should you desire to have a luxury vehicle, a big house, designer clothes or travel the world… let it be because it is your desire, your dream not because you want to impress others.

On the other hand, should you desire to live a modest lifestyle free of worldly possessions, again…. your choice to make! Never allow anyone to make you feel because you possess less worldly possessions that you are less than any other who has more. Some of the happiest and most loving people in the world are those who do not have two pennies to rub together.

How many of you right now wish you did not have to wonder how you were going to pay the mortgage/rent, car note or buy groceries? There are some who never set foot in a grocery store or visit a market… why, because they grow their own food, or they make their own clothing. What matters most is being true to thine self, love, peace, and happiness…. Please "don't fake it until you make it," embrace where you are and let your light shine through the goodness of your blessings, put in the work – your time is near.

Ask yourself, is my lifestyle authentic? Am I creating a lifestyle created due to my triumph and growth or is this lifestyle created solely to upstage my competition?

Use the following journal page to write your thoughts.

Journal Page

3

Luxury Isn't For The Faint At Heart

The comparison with the couple, "The Jones' was illustrated with all intentions to help you realize – much in this life isn't at all as it appears. It is more about your perception. Just as your perception of others may be far left - the same goes for you, as others perceive you and your lifestyle.

Society defines High maintenance as "someone who demands a lot of attention (much is required for their upkeep). How others will perceive your desire for a luxurious lifestyle or those who prefer a more simplistic lifestyle is again all about perception. Understand, the purpose of reading this book is to broaden your horizons. Is it conceivable that many would live a happier more fulfilled life if there was more focus on needs and less on wants?

Having the finer things in life is great, it is absolutely wonderful. I doubt anyone is dreaming to live an impoverished lifestyle. Yet, at what price does it cost emotionally and financially to live lavishly? Is it causing friction within households? Is it disrupting families because there are those who feel the grass may be greener on the other side of the fence?

Are you working overtime continuously to afford these same pleasures as The Jones - unable to really enjoy life because you are dead tired once you get home? The next day, the rat race continues, back to the hustle and bustle of your day to day.

The finer things in life, cost and often will cost you BIG. No, it most certainly is not for the faint at heart. It comes with long hours, long weeks, long months, and long years. You see it all the time, celebs at various shows – from one city to another city. Many cannot maintain a healthy relationship with their spouse or children. Yes, someone must be present, and someone has to provide. The big elephant in the room that must be addressed, what type of lifestyle do we as a family desire to live? What commitment have I vowed to my spouse?

And if that lifestyle requires you to work majority of the 365 days in a year and your spouse and/or family agree, cool. But, if not… someone has some reevaluating to do. If you're working 60 hours a week equates to lack of quality time and you are now neglecting your mate emotional needs, are you still aligned with your vows?

For me, do not give me the mansion on the hill only to leave me lonely. Give me the condo close to the ocean and let us travel the world. What is it that you and your family can honestly live with? My happiness does not necessarily equate to yours and yours to mine.

Lifestyle, lifestyle, lifestyle. I cannot emphasize it enough!!! The goal is for you to create a lifestyle you will be proud to call your own. Creating tunnel vision is essential, inspiration is necessary. We all should be inspired by others, but what type of inspiration?

Should that inspiration solely consist of tangible things or should you also be inspired to love your fellow man or help others less fortunate? Should that inspiration come by way of pursuit of education or by developing a love for art or creating a movement for some type of change? Inspiration comes from many, many avenues… all are not found on the same street. Where will you find inspiration and from whom or what source? What will it mean for your lifestyle? How can you inspire others? Yes, this world is constantly changing and if we do not change, we will remain stagnant.

But guess what, you get to decide in what manner you will change… will you follow the crowd and go right, or will you instead make a left? Will you walk the path of the straight and narrow by being the leader of your own destiny? Growing is not all about monetary wealth, we can be rich in many other areas of our lives. You do realize this, please tell me that you do?!

Throughout the years, I've learned to pray not for monetary value but instead for favor because favor can reach places that money is not invited. Favor has a long stretch in its arms. I pray for favor when it comes to those that I love – each morning I pray that God will give my spouse, my family, friends and loved ones favor in the sight of God and man. Favor for my grandchildren in the classrooms and favor amongst their classmates, favor that their teachers will want to pour into them knowledge that far exceeds the expected curriculum – favor that their classmates will want to do good towards them and not cause hurt feelings nor harm.

Think about it… when you favor someone you put them first; they are important to you. You make certain they are well taken care of – that their needs are met. There is no money put before you that can tempt you when you favor someone. Favor shields, it promotes, it enrich-es…favor moves you and takes you places!

With that being said, live a little… enjoy the beauty of what life has to offer outside of your four walls: office or home. Remember, if you must work hard…. "Don't work to simply pay bills!" Your primary goal should be to live within your own means and create a lifestyle based upon your goals – crossing accomplished goals off your list one by one. This will create less stress and more time for enjoyment with those you love and embrace, for far too many never received the opportunity to get one more day with a loved one. Tomorrow is not promised, we all have an expiration date.

With age, many begin to view life with a new lens. I have already lived almost half of my life and I look back and wonder where the time has gone as I am sure many of you do as well. I cannot change the decisions made in my younger days, but I can most certainly control the direction I will take for the rest of my best days ahead. I proclaim!

In time, you realize some things that once mattered aren't as important to you any longer; the past relationships with others who never deserved your time to begin with, the competitiveness with the next man or woman… it all seems more like child's play anymore. Family comes to the forefront of your decision making – you are now concerned about how those decisions will impact your family in the long haul. You now research financial investments with caution, frivolous spending and impulse shopping tendencies are eliminated.

You find yourself becoming more informative about your surroundings and the world around you. Wants verses needs, this is a good place to draw the line in the sand. Do not cross them, do not get them con-fused. Even, if it means that you must literally sit down and write out what your wants and needs consist of. It is necessary for some, to maintain that healthy discipline to see growth.

You want that new car, but is it a necessity? "If it isn't broke, why fix it?" We have all heard this expression, right? Do you really need that higher car note? Yes, let us 100% enjoy the finer things in life but only if it isn't going to cause you to struggle. What fun is it if you must cringe every month when it is time to transfer funds or mail that check for that new car?

Please be careful that you do not want so much that you work your-self into exhaustion over things that are not enhancing your lifestyle for the betterment of you. Instead, those same wants that now have been purchased are collecting dust over in a corner…no face value, ultimately a total waste.

There are some goal driven individuals that only work hard for an allotted amount of time, their sole purpose is to accomplish a particular goal. It could be to obtain the down payment for a new house, or payoff an existing loan or begin that business that you have always aspired to achieve.

You don't have to explain to anyone except those you love why you are working so hard. My only caution let there be purpose behind it. Please know, the money you earn while here on earth will be left here on earth. Please leave time to actually live your life and enjoy the fruits of your labor.

What are your family's lifestyle goals? Will you now focus more on your needs verses your wants? Does everything in your life have to be "over-the-top" or can you appreciate the simplistic things in life?

Use the following journal page to write your thoughts.

Journal Page

Simplicities

"There is beauty in simplicity," everything does not have to be over the top always ladies and gentlemen. It is alright to let your hair down and to dress down sometimes. You do not always have to be in suit, tie, or heels. I joke often and say that I was "born in heels" due to my love of heels. I just feel as a woman it provides that extra "something" that makes you feel sexy. However, with age I can appreciate the need to wear sneakers or flats. Although honestly, I can walk better in heels than flats. Go figure! Ladies, speaking of heels. If you cannot wear four- or five-inch heels, please stick to a comfortable heel size because it will definitely show up in your walk. The goal is to walk as stallions walk. Head held high, shoulders up and one foot in front of the other. It's the confidence when you walk. The look of nervousness is not displayed as sexy, so please again please stick to a suitable heel for your comfort level.

Speaking of letting your hair down. My son as a child would beg me not to get dressed up, he wanted to see me in sweats, t-shirts, and sneakers sometimes. For him, I would do it because we loved going to the park, but he did not understand why I did not want to do it while going to the mall. The mall was the fashion show back in the day. You dressed to go to the mall. You never knew "who" you would bump into or at least that was my perception of mall days.

Isn't it ironic that it appears on your worst days you tend to bump into someone that you don't want to see you looking your worst? It is always someone you have not seen in forever, but sometimes wondered where they were or how they were doing. My parents insisted we do not leave the house with our hair uncombed and looking a mess! After all, they felt that their children were a representation of them. I agree one hundred percent. I dislike seeing parents appearing well groomed and their children not even their hair brushed or combed because it is totally a reflection of you.

A lot of what you see in others has to do with their upbringing and how they were raised as children. If there was a lot of laughter, adventure, etc. in the home often, children will demonstrate the same in their parenting as adults. Stop to smell the flowers, no matter what environment you are in. There is always a place for a flower even if it must be placed in a pot. However, if you are a homeowner find a place to have some live plants in your home. Granted, everyone was not born with a green thumb so make sure you consult the nursery for a low maintenance plant if gardening just is not your thing.

Skin, hair, and body - We all not only want to feel our best, but we want to look our best. One of the things I have learned over the years is to stop buying every advertisement that you see.

Sometimes you only need the basics. I also discovered that prescribed medications were not the best solutions for my skin. Sure, I tried various products but to be honest the best solution for me was to avoid stress, never sleep in my makeup, allow my skin to breathe free of makeup (I love color on my skin), exfoliating several times a week, moisturizing with oil free (non-comedogenic; won't clog pores) lotions and SPF (sun protection factor; protect against sun rays), rest and water. The latter, I honestly still struggle with but am aware that they are essential for maintaining your youthfulness. Men, this is essential for you as well to exfoliate your skin, moisturize, rest, exercise, and water. Do not allow your girlfriend/wives to sleep in makeup. If my husband sees that I am falling asleep with my makeup on, he will wake me and remind me that I need to wash my makeup off.

Ladies, great makeup begins and ends with great skin underneath it. If you have pimples on your skin, it will still protrude with makeup. I have used drug store makeup before, there is nothing wrong with it just make sure that it is one that promotes healthy skin. There is actually makeup with beneficial ingredients to promote healthier skin, please look for this not just something to help with coverage. I feel a woman looks the most youthful with less makeup than a face full of makeup. Currently, I wear a department store makeup foundation & concealer (2 in 1); it is a liquid and I use minimal. I apply with a wand brush and use highlight shimmer on my face to enhance my natural glows on most days I keep it simple (my preference).

My hat goes off to those who can use twenty techniques of contouring, mixing colors, the eyebrows and all of that. I am sorry, but that is not for me. I am pretty simple when it comes to makeup. Sometimes, I will add lashes which is quite the task (not quite mastered), I will do a little contour on my cheekbones, add blush and highlight, mascara, always some type of lip color, maybe eye liner sometimes, it depends on the occasion. I know some women who are completely natural and have never worn makeup, again "there's beauty in simplicity." I do love color, but I can totally appreciate and respect all-natural beautiful Queens. Salute.

Speaking of falling asleep…what do you fall asleep to sleep to at night? Is it the television, music, audio books, sermons or natures sounds? Years ago, I implemented sound machines into my nightly regimen of falling asleep. Today, both my husband and I take gummy melatonin; we both suffer from insomnia often, we also sleep to nature sounds (most often the sound of rain) for a peaceful night's rest. It also helps couples to really try to avoid going to bed angry. Let us bow our heads and pray. This does not always happen for most of us, unfortunately.

However, please try not to go to bed angry. Instead, promote healthy sleep habits.

If you want to count sheep in your sleep, change your sheets. The key to "good sleep" also is to wash your linen on the regular. I have also found that finding a nice linen fragrance for your bed works wonders also. Give it a try. Thread count is also important, designer sheets I have found also are of better quality. Wait for the sales folks, and sleep tight at night. Deep pocket sheets prevent the sheets from slipping through-out the night. Ladies, if you want to avoid placing a head wrap on your head. Invest in silk pillowcases. Silk pillowcases do not strip the natural oils from your hair. Men, I am sure your hair could also benefit from this (black, white, or deep chocolate would be great masculine colors).

If you want the things you invest in to last, washing in cold water prevents a lot of your items from fading and it keeps the integrity of your fabrics together. Clothes that I want to last, I do not place in the dryer. I hang them on my shower rod in my guest bathroom and allow them to air dry overnight. My clothing will last me forever if I do not donate them. I have practiced this since my son was a young boy and I now have grandchildren, so yes, a very long time. You work hard, so take care of your investments. This is a great way to help you take care of everything you purchase; you have invested your hard-earned money into this item, make it last! The same applies to shoes and everything else; clean them often inside and out, store them properly do not just throw them all on the floor of your closets or room.

Sweet smells. Everyone loves a great smelling man or woman, right? I know I do. I learned a secret right before the pandemic hit. It was not even intentional - just a little something that I stumbled across. The portable perfume bottle roll on and sprays are perfect for travel "yes," but they are also perfect to try new fragrances without breaking the bank. I purchased maybe four bottles of travel size perfume bottles it has been almost a year and I have only completely emptied one bottle. I wear perfume or a body mist spray daily, but when you invest in multiple bottles you use less of your favorite perfumes.

Make sure you have fragrances that are nighttime appropriate and daytime friendly. Warmer perfumes I tend to prefer for the nights and the lighter fresh scents I love during the daytime. This works for me. What I love about the travel size is that I can carry with me on an outing to refreshen my perfume or cologne. Ladies, it is a must to add to any of your existing collections. Please whatever you do, do not substitute perfume for a shower, overpowering use of any scent is an instant headache for most people around you. Hit those key spots; neck (one side only), wrists (one wrist, rub both wrists together) and ankle (only one side) ladies. The key to applying to your ankle is when you walk the perfume scent will rise into the air. Men, I cannot help you there, but I would imagine that the chest would be a great area. It may burn on the neck if you shave but perhaps behind the neck right below the hairline would be a great place for your cologne.

Some may already know the keys to applying fragrances to the body. However, you cannot presume that everyone was taught or has learned this. Some just spray all over their body and/or clothing. The wrong thing to do. It is a sure way to waste perfume and to prolong and overlap scents. Always spray on person and not your article of clothing please. This is how my perfume lasts, purchasing multiple scents and applying to my body only.

You should have a solid color in your closets; black, white, brown, off-white, red (you get the idea). You can mix and match. You do not have to have a closet full of clothes to look nice. Make sure your clothes are clean, ironed and coordinated and you are good to go.

Hair. Hair. Ladies and our hair. May the Lord help us! What I can tell you is, get some great conditioner that works for you in your life. This is the secret I have found. I have also found that I have made the mistake far too often with entrusting everyone with their hands in my hair. No more! Ladies study your own hair. Learn what works for it and if you can and have the skills to maintain your hair, do so. If you need to go to the salon once a month or for some ladies, I know it is a treat for themselves to go weekly, biweekly, or monthly. I am not her. I do my own hair most of the time unless it is time for a cut, or there is a skill that I know that I cannot do.

Otherwise, I am conditioning my hair biweekly and not stripping my hair with shampoos of its natural oils. It is important that you get your hair trimmed and do not over process. I am still learning this hair thing, but as I mentioned earlier sleeping with a silk pillowcase does wonders for your hair and skin. Make sure you wash them often. Color. Great hair begins with a nice color. Have a little fun and step outside of your comfort zones ladies. I have had a lot of fun with both long and short styles; clip in extensions and weaves but I must say my favorites are my own hair and a good sew-in. One secret that saves times and money is a U-part wig, these wigs are the most natural wigs. It resembles a sew-in when worn but it seamlessly blends in with your natural hair and can be sewn to braided hair or clipped in. I have tried both.

Ladies and gentlemen stop keeping your grooming secrets to your-self. Help someone else out at least sometimes if you see them struggling. Do not be a bully and talk about someone who has not mastered the skills of grooming, instead share your pearls of wisdom with them. It boosts self confidence in others when they can look and feel good about themselves.

Treat yourself and others with respect. I respect my body and I in-sist that others respect my body as well. I have never allowed a man to mishandle me intimately in the bedroom. It was a pearl of wisdom my grandmother shared with me as a youth. To date, I still have all of my female organs. Annual wellness exams are essential. In addition, I have never abused alcohol or drugs. For those in the struggle who are recovering with addictions, my prayers are with you. You can beat it! I do drink on occasion socially, but responsibly. Respect yourself enough to care about what happens to you. Ask yourself this…

What are some things learned over the years that I can share with someone that I know struggles in a certain area and can benefit from my sharing? What are the things that I did not know, but will now introduce into my routine? Am I taking care of my well-being to the best of my ability? In what ways do I show respect for myself and to others?

Use the following journal page to write your thoughts.

Journal Page

5

The "A" List

"othing should make you; you should make it!" Truth be told, I have received the most compliments when I have not worn any designer brand fashions at all nor dressed my home in designer décor. Do you really need someone's name on your back or in your home for you to feel secure or good about yourself? I think not…

Yes, I absolutely do believe in treating myself to the finer things, but I have never set out to shop exclusively at particular stores or designer brands to impress others. For starters, I never wanted to look nor dress like everyone else. I have always had a desire to be different, set apart from the rest. Although, other opinions mattered in the past - to have my own individuality has always been more appealing to me.

This statement is also true of my home. With experience, I have learned to never purchase complete room packages from one furniture store but instead buy individual pieces from various stores. I imagine it would feel awful to walk into another person's home and their interior looks the same as your home. I will never know what that awkward moment would feel like, because it's something that I do not exercise within my own household.

I've always admired homes with unique curb appeal and architectural design instead of the standard cookie cutter communities. There is something to be said for individuals who set themselves apart from the crowd. Daring to be different, shows one's creativeness and zest for life. Do not allow yourself to feel obligated to follow the crowd or submit to the norm simply to fit in.

Over the years, I've had the pleasure of knowing several individuals who loved to shop in thrift stores or as some call them secondhand stores. Yet, those individuals were viewed as "fashionistas" simply because of their style. Little did they know, they weren't at all obsessive "followers of fashion" to the contrary, they were simply creating their own fashion trend.

Ask yourself, what brand do you prefer? Do you prefer your own brand or the brand of the crowd pleasers?

Please do not misconceive my questions. I too enjoy some of the latest fashions and trends. However, the difference is that I am not obsessed nor are they "must haves." These are secondary choices. I allow my eyes to choose anything I desire and unfortunately, for me "most often" they are the most expensive things money can buy. Reality check: Most of the things I want…at this time, I cannot afford financially because the price tags are pretty steep.

Let me just keep it real, I think I was born with expensive taste. My husband and I have been out shopping and without me even knowing the price, I somehow tend to choose the most expensive items. We laugh now because it has become so common that it is hard to refute.

Here is a funny story I must share. My uncle invited my cousin and I on a road trip, this was many years ago when I was a young girl. We traveled to visit some of his military friends, great people, lovely couple. We went to dinner that evening and somehow, I missed that the entire table ordered the salad buffet. When it was my turn to order, I ordered a steak, potato, and a salad. It was the first item that caught my eye on the menu. Someone chimed in with laughter, "someone has taught her well." Needless to say, I wasn't refused my steak dinner.

It was not that my parents instilled me to worship material things because our faith wouldn't allow that to be so. However, it was the value of "quality" investing in things that had value. Spending your hard-earned money on things that were built to last and maintaining your goods to last you many years to come. Exposing me to living a life of enjoyment; laughter and fulfillment. It did not require an abundance but if you were fortunate to find a great deal get all you can (store up).

You know the story of "the ant and the grasshopper" how the ant stored up his food for the winter and the grasshopper is left begging for food come winter. Do you want this to be you? Or do you prefer to be prepared? Preparation is key; it consists of investing in quality verses quantity and storing up. In today's society, unfortunately there are few things that are built to last. For consumers, things are built to keep you coming back because what you purchase is more likely to require replacement because it wears out and doesn't last.

Experience has taught me to not attach myself to things I simply "like" or tolerate. When you hear the word "like" how do you define it? Is it safe to say, you feel "it's okay, it is tolerable?" Yet, when you hear the word "love" oh my goodness "you absolutely have to have it and cannot live without it!" Big difference, right? Now, do you see where I am going with this? When you hear the word "love" it's "the best thing since sliced bread." You must have it, right!!!

Try this… every time you buy something that you absolutely "love" donates something you simply "like" out of your home or closet. If your home is your "refuge;" a place of tranquility – will you apply the principles discussed in this chapter and take the time to invest in yourself and your home with a new perspective?

Or will you continue to allow "the chaos of this world to invade your peace?" Isn't your home, the place which holds most of your identity as well as your loved ones, priceless memories, home furnishings, clothing, intimate apparel, handbags, shoe collection, family photos, important documents, tools, vehicles, jewelry, music collections, etc.

If this is what stores most of the things you value, why not allow it to perform at its best for you…

What is it that you love? What are you tolerating instead of loving? What do you deem as of value in your life? What are you willing to let go of? Are you ready to rid your lifestyle of clutter? If so, let us get ready to organize!!!

Use the following journal page to write your thoughts.

Journal Page

6

Are We Clear To Enter?

*M*any know that there are certain areas of your home which should always be kept tidy. In my opinion, these areas are bathrooms, kitchens and living rooms (common areas). If someone stopped by your home unannounced would you be embarrassed to allow them into your home, into your bathroom or kitchen? Would you have to pick up toys and shoes from your floors?

I'll go a little bit further; it actually begins the moment your residence is within a person's view. Whether it is your driveway or the entry to your front door – a person forms an impression from there. Your curb appeal should reflect your personality, whether you are conservative or bold, modern, or traditional. You don't have to be a homeowner to show pride in where you reside – it should be an honor to maintain a residence even if you are not the homeowner because the owner has entrusted you with their property to maintain the upkept of it.

The media has exposed the compulsive hoarders throughout America through video and episode television shows. I am a firm believer, that this is a disorder. Hoarders in my opinion, require professional assistance. However, I am not referring to hoarders here. I am referring to mentally stable, healthy individuals, capable of maintaining their households.

Personally, I have always been able to identify when I am emotion-ally not handling a situation well because my house starts to be in disarray. If I can function in that environment, it is a clear sign to me that I have bigger fish to fry. Yet, once I've overcome whatever obstacle – it becomes completely unbearable to me to see things out of place.

Ask yourself, the following questions:

Is my disarray due to situational depression or stress? Is my untidy dwelling due to laziness?

Am I stretched too thin and need to prioritize, to clean?

Everything you purchase should have a place for its use, if not… why are you purchasing something without a place to park? Will this purchase be left idling around your home? Leave it in the store if it serves no purpose in your life. This will help to alleviate clutter.

Alleviating clutter in your life, will bring clarity. Clarity will bring about progression, you will soon begin to see growth. All of these things work hand in hand. Connect the dots and allow your perception of how you decide to live your life begin to move.

The mess in your life, does not always equate to tangible things. It could be baggage that you have been holding on to and not letting go of that is now interfering with your peace. It could be a relationship with a girlfriend or romantic interest that is causing a mess. It is time to clean house and I mean clean house good. For my over thirty folks and especially, over forty- and fifty-year old's – how much longer will it take for you to empty the nest of clutter in your life and gain some real clarity, pearls of wisdom on how you will live your future. C'mon you are closer to the finish line than not. How many more lessons needs repeating? That is right, none. You learned that lesson, right?

I believe in the "quarterly cleaning," those closest to me know this is me! For years and years, I have had this organizational system – as each season enters, I pack up the previous season.

Granted, we honestly do not have drastic seasonal changes here in "sunny Florida" where I reside.

However, it does not matter. Religiously, I have practiced this to help keep my mind clutter free.

You have heard "one man's junk, is another's man treasure?" Well, donations are always welcomed. There are plenty of people in your local community who will appreciate a helping hand. How frustrating is it, to know you have a favorite shirt or pants but cannot seem to find it anywhere in your closet because you still have your summer and winter clothes mixed together? I honestly have found that an organized closet keeps me organized all around. Being able to see what you have within reach is crucial to functionality of my everyday living. It makes getting ready in the mornings easier. It has also saved me a ton of money because I am no longer purchasing too many of the same items in similar style or color.

If storage is a problem (lack of space) perhaps try buying wardrobe trunks that are now once again in high demand. Suit bags are another solution. I use suit bags to store my party dresses separately from my everyday clothing. The same goes with your shoes, you can also store away shoes you do not wear every day. When that invite arrives in the mail or the announcement that your niece is getting married or your favorite artist group is in town, you will now know exactly where to go in your closet for the perfect outfit and if it is not found there…. Well, there is your perfect excuse to now go shopping for the occasion.

If you have begun practicing any of my suggestions listed in the previous chapters – you are well on your way to having a functional, multi-purpose household which will ultimately lead to a "lifestyle you will be proud to call your own."

I ask you now…. Is it safe to enter your home? Are you void of mess? Or would you like for us to continue tip toeing around… pretending we cannot see the clutter which remains ….

How organized is your place of refuge? Is there any place in your home could benefit from organizing? If your home is in disarray, what do you feel has caused this?

Use the following journal page to write your thoughts.

Journal Page

7

The Exclusive Class

*M*ost people love bargains and will rush to get a great deal. What do you consider a deal? Again, this is all about lifestyle.... I am a newlywed and with a new marriage came bonus children, which I proudly accept-ed. Well, baby girl was visiting one summer, and I was running low on hand soap, typically there are certain soaps that I purchase simply because they last forever it seems. I told baby girl that "we were going to a department store to pick up some hand soap." I felt this was a perfect opportunity to teach her about "quality verses quantity."

I explained, "I can go to the local discounted store and purchase five bottles of hand soap for the price of this one, however those same five bottles will be gone in a matter of a few weeks.

Or I could buy one bottle of "quality soap" (always wait for sale time and stock up) which will last me months. The more expensive brand hand soap not only smells better, but it is also better for your skin and lasts longer; these products are made with "the haves" in mind not "the have nots," therefore shopping in the same stores will afford you the fine products as well.

The same applies for room sprays (department stores room sprays will last forever). Now tell me, which of the two is the better deal? Lifestyle choices.... Everything is about the decisions we make now; you can change how your lifestyle will look for the future beginning now with something as simple as hand soap. Remember, quality lasts and will save you dollars in the long run – the wealthy are already aware of these shopper secrets, it is time you join the club.

Wait for the sales. I have one even better for you, there are certain department store credit cards which offer additional huge savings when you purchase products by credit. Well, just because you purchase on credit does not mean you have to let it incur interest. Pay immediately on that same credit card after you have made your purchase. You leave a happy customer with great discounts and zero interest on your store credit card. While in stores, if online coupons are available share your wealth of information with others, trust me it is appreciated. And in return, in the future you will not hesitate to ask others where they are finding their resourceful coupon sites.

Are you open to change and anxious to begin making your money work smarter not harder for your lifestyle? Are you concerned with being labeled by others because you choose to invest in quality verses quantity?

Use the following journal page to write your thoughts.

Journal Page

8

A Diamond In The Rough

I cannot speak for you, but as for me and my household "we work hard for the money!" I believe in pampering myself every opportunity possible; spas, getaways, and fine dining. I love entertainment, especially if it includes LIVE music. I see nothing wrong with living life!

Why not enjoy the same luxuries as those in higher income brackets; after all, we contribute to the growth of the economy as well. Who works to pay bills only? I am sorry but it bears repeating until you hear me! The finest hotels and restaurants just do it for me every time; it is my ultimate pleasure.

Now, let us discuss my dislikes…the things that I do not like. I dis-like receiving bills with balances in the mailbox, or bill collectors calling my phone, these are my dislikes. You begin to learn patience when your goal is to become debt free. It will not happen overnight unless you are fortunate to come into a financial windfall. Therefore, for most of us… it must begin with a process.

My secret to creating balance and being able to experience the occasional luxuries – is all about timing! 'Timing truly is everything – booking four-and five-star hotels/resorts are at their best value during off peak seasons and avoiding holidays. Once visited, I have appreciated less traffic from other visitors during these off-peak seasons. Always comparison shop other websites, ask for discounts (i.e., military, auto club membership, employment, or discount codes). There is no shame in asking for discounts wherever you patronize.

Being sociable goes a long way also, don't be afraid to ask guests once at a resort "what source did they use to book their reservation?" Often, you hear of discounted sites you've never heard of. If there is a particular hotel chain you visit often due to work or pleasure, enroll in their rewards membership club and be on the "lookout" for their email alerts of discounted or earned free night stays – be sure to capitalize on these point systems.

Many hotels are now participating in day passes. What does this mean? It means many of the hotels that are typically the most expensive will allow you to visit for the day at an extremely low price to enjoy all the hotel's amenities. This is available in cities throughout this country. I recently visited one on my last birthday and let me just say that I felt like a celebrity, not only did they provide me with a free drink, but the pool menu was available, the hot tub, lazy river, and shower room. These make perfect gifts and great for those celebrating anniversaries.

Embrace where you are! Your decision making from today forward can make a tremendous impact on the lifestyle you create for your tomorrow.

How did this chapter benefit you, what is your takeaway?

Use the following journal page to write your thoughts.

Journal Page

9

The Elite Class

The current buzz in "major" cities throughout the country are restaurants offering fine dining at "discounted fixed menu prices." De-pending on the city, it could last for a week or months long. Imagine indulging in fine cuisine and experiencing the ambiance of some of the top restaurants, stepping out for a night out in your town.

Imagine being served dishes prepared by top chefs preparing meals to tantalize your palate. You need an excuse for date night with your significant other, girl's night or to simply treat yourself? Well, it is a perfect opportunity to jazz it up and step out! Search the entertainment weekly section of your local city news and surely, you will find some of the latest new spots to try.

Every year for the past couple of years my husband and I have tried different restaurants at resorts and at restaurants where it is merely impossible to get a table even with a reservation in advance. The most memorable one by far was two years ago at a resort, it had a roof top fireplace, and we were able to witness the nightly fireworks on display from the restaurant's large windows, a pure delight.

These fine dining specials offer impeccable service, you are treated like royalty. Typically, most cities will begin late summer around August when the children are back approaching school days. I will never forget one server "thanked my husband for bringing me to him." To this day, we still laugh about that – we were tickled at the quality of service and mannerism of the server. It is said that servers at "an elite fine dining restaurant can make more than six figures a year" therefore, your satisfaction matters.

I know I became so frustrated constantly requesting the manager to complain about a meal or the service – it was a refreshing change to provide a "compliment" instead of "complaint!" As I stated, many cities offer dining weeks or months at discounted prices. At times, this option may be unavailable but please do not despair instead resort to your favorite discount websites and remember to register your email for restaurant member rewards (their member rewards notifications you will soon welcome).

Have you ever considered instead of paying for a costly dinner priced menu item trying a new restaurant for breakfast, brunch, lunch, or happy hour (half off appetizers) and discounted drinks? Which can you try for the first time or enjoy more of in your lifestyle? By doing so, you can really check the place out without breaking the bank and without being disappointed if it did not meet your expectations. Considering the cost is also less pricey than your dinner cost, this is a great choice for a first date…choose brunch or lunch. Typically, the crowds are smaller, and it will serve as a perfect opportunity to get to know this wonderful individual.

Open your horizons and invite your taste palate to the elite. Close your eyes and begin to savor the moments to come…

Are you ready to become a dining rewards member? Your mouth is at work constantly, why not treat it to the finest.

Use the following journal page to write your thoughts.

Journal Page

10

Shower Me

*A*s a native Floridian naturally, I am drawn to anything water related. The shower is my place where I gather myself. I would hear of people taking thirty-minute showers and I always thought of it to be a senseless waste of good water. However, with life constantly throwing blows… I have found it truly a place of escape and meditation.

How often do others interfere with you when you are in the show-er? Typically, no one does. Therefore, it has now become my space of meditation. If you have not tried this, please do. Allow the water to rain down on you from head to toe, close your eyes and massage the water continually over your face, neck, and shoulders. You know all those places where pressure of stress builds.

You decorate every other part of your house. Pay close attention to the things in your master en suite or family bathroom. Let this be your place of Zen. Let it become your tropical paradise. Start piece by piece replacing items, towels, robes, floral arrangements, wall pictures. Search magazines and online photographs to gather new ideas for your new spa. Yes, I like to think of my bathroom as my spa. I love treating myself to spa soaps, essential oils, and other must have necessities that you find when you are on vacation.

Avoid excessive clutter of products (i.e., makeup, hair, skin products). Keep in mind, it is always about keeping only items that you absolutely love. If you are currently using a skin care product that is proving effective, why replace? The same goes for laundry and dish detergent. Avoid replacing products every time you shop. Instead, find a product and stick to it. Especially, with hair. Ladies, we can easily over excess when it comes to hair care products. Many of you have enough to start your very own online store.

When vacationing my first inkling is to race into the bathroom to smell the soaps, shampoo, and conditioner. If I love it, I will go online and purchase larger bottles upon my return home. I found one of my all-time favorites while visiting Times Square in New York City. To this day, it is still one of my top faves. Once upon a time, I had an entire bottom drawer full of soaps, lotions, and shampoo/conditioners that I had left over from hotels I previously visited. That is always an option because let's face it if you're only staying for a few days… there's always leftover in those bottles. Treat yourself.

Where is your spa? Have you created such a place for you indoors or outdoors? If so, are you maintaining it and utilizing it on a regular basis?

Use the following journal page to write your thoughts.

Journal Page

11

Who's The Boss?

What do you intend to do with the information received throughout this book? Please share, do not keep all this knowledge to yourself! Who is the boss? You are! You are the boss if you take control of you and your family's lifestyle now.

Are you dressing for success? Do you realize sales are your best friend? I really dislike using the word designer instead I prefer using the word quality. In my son's younger school age days, his father and I would shop for him every season. In winter he would receive a winter wardrobe of clothes and shoes, then spring, so on and so forth. As we would enter the stores, my eyes would lead me straight to the sales rack. That is where I considered the great deals to be found.

Yes, he had designer clothes but surprisingly, my final total was no more than what you would pay at your local discounted store. That is the misconception that so many have that because people buy designer clothes that they are paying top dollar. Granted, some really do pay regular price, but I have better things to do with my funds than to make someone else wealthy. I would rather keep more of my coins to invest in so that one day I will have something to leave for my children's children.

You have heard of old money. Well, old money often came from real estate, land and investments. "Old money," sustained their wealth throughout generations because the principles were also passed down; the knowledge of how they established and grew their wealth. Stop wearing your salary and instead live in it, own it, or lease it out to others but by all means, do not wear it on your back unless it is your own brand. We lead by example. The most important is that you are clean. If you purchase a shirt that is $1.00, and you are clean and you have someone who is wearing $1,000 jacket who is covered in dirt, who do you think will get noticed first?

It is the same with your home? If you are currently not able to purchase new furniture take pride in what you have. Keep it clean. People can appreciate cleanliness. If your workload prevents you from doing the housework yourself, sacrifice and hire someone to come in to assist weekly or monthly but please do not allow your home to lead you into a dark place. As Christians, ask yourself does God dwell in filth? I think not. Consider this when you allow your lifestyle to get away from you. As children, my older brother and I had chores and trust those chores better had been completed by the time our mother arrived home.

I do not understand why so many parents have allowed their children to feel entitled. Why can't your child wash a dish? Why can't they do their own laundry? I taught my son at a young age how to separate the dark from light colors and how to wash and fold? We are doing this new generation a disservice by not instilling in them the same principles.

Granted these days, I will pay for convenience because my time is valuable. As you should also consider yours valuable. However, I do feel there are still principles that our children and grandchildren, nieces, nephews, and friend's children need instilled in them. Basic principles that did us no harm. For example, how to make up our beds when we awake in the mornings. To this day, my older brother and I still do this. It was instilled in us at an early age. We feel uncomfortable to come home to an unmade bed. Basic to live by. Think about for a moment some of the things your parents insist that you did around the house.

What can you instill in this generation that benefited you in yours?

What chores will you implement into your household for your family?

Use the following journal page to write your thoughts.

Journal Page

12

Friend Or Foe

You are most definitely the company that you keep… choose your friends wisely. I was never one to need a lot of friends, but one who could attract many because of my kind spirit. It was the strange, unexplainable behaviors that I could no longer justify that made it clear I had plenty of wolves in sheep's clothing lurking around me with their mouths snaring at me.

Do not be upset, disappointed or make a fuss. Do not automatically view this as the devil because God must approve it all. God allowed it to happen to you for a reason. Do you understand this? I cannot lie, this was a hard pill to swallow for a long time. I felt as though there were people close to me who knew of some of the most devastating things I have experienced in life so why would they be envious or why would they even be jealous?

You know why…. It was not the failure; it was not the devastation. It was the triumph! I got up! It did not break me. In fact, it elevated me to new heights it motivated me to soar higher. It encouraged me to rise above the hate. Experience has been my best teacher. It taught me that when I surrounded myself with a circle of like-minded individuals who had the same zest for life, hunger for spiritual growth and wanted to break generational curses… I became unstoppable! Things that once moved me could no longer get a response, at all. Growth!

What have you outgrown? Have you outgrown the need to be right? Who is your circle of friends? Are you open to broadening your mind to new adventures and crowds you would not necessarily mingle with?

Use the following journal page to write your thoughts

Journal Page

13

Unbothered

Be unmoved and totally unbothered, by the antics of people who you have had discord with from the past. Don't let them interfere with your newfound peace. You have prayed. You have received deliverance from your past sins. You put in the work and worked extremely hard to turn over a new leaf, a new chapter in your life. Do not allow anyone to take you out of character simply to prove a point. Do not entertain pettiness. You are so much bigger than a petty response.

"It is, what it is" therefore, you cannot change anyone. You cannot make others have morals and values. You cannot make another human live up to the principles that you have set forth for your life. You continue to work on yourself, always treating others with kindness but please stay woke. Do not be deceived by manipulation. My greatest lesson learned was to stop giving all of me to those who only want to give me less of them. Invest your valued time into those who invest in you and want to see you winning in life.

My life changed completely when I set boundaries in all of my relationships; personal, business and family. It honestly has saved my life. There is no need for an explanation to anyone why you cannot do something unless you feel a need to explain. Learn to say "no" respect-fully but without guilt or allowing others to condemn you for not wanting to be a part of something.

Who knows your body better than you do? No one. You should

know better than anyone how your body responds to the environment, stress, exercise and what you put into it. Therefore, this also means you should know your stress levels. Stress is not good for anyone. Make it a great day every day on purpose because you have made a conscious decision to not allow the behaviors of anyone else to cause your mood to waiver. When you awake each morning, arise with thanksgiving that you are among "the land of the living." So many others did not make it to see another day.

Soar like an eagle beautiful one. Recognize the beauty within your-self, and within your lifestyle. You are now investing in something that you can be proud to call your own. Not by the definitions of how anyone else sees your life, but instead by how you have defined your lifestyle for you! Are you happy? I certainly hope so. If not, why are you waiting? "Time waits for no man."

Do you feel guilt when declining an invitation? What is your morning mood typically? Have you set boundaries with others? Can you honestly say that you know your body? Do you take heed to warning signs of stress? Do you respond to pettiness?

Use the following journal page to write your thoughts.

Journal Page

14

Worthy

Whether you are single or married please know that you are worthy. You are worthy to have a voice. Do not ever allow another human to silence your voice. I feel that is the most degrading thing a human can do to another. Everyone has a right to voice their opinion when in relationship with another person. The relationship can be totally platonic, it does not matter. We all have a voice on how we want others to treat us.

Set expectations! Exercise what those expectations are. Many do not understand what is expected of them from other people. If we are adults, why is it so difficult to communicate as adults? One of the most valuable lessons I have learned the past few years is respect. Respect is everything. When you respect another individual there are simply lines that you absolutely will not cross because you respect them enough to not disrespect them. There are some regrets I have in this area.

I hate and I know hate is a strong word that should not be used. Honestly, I hate that I allowed myself to lower my behavior to another person. I urge you to please when you have a disagreement with someone – watch your words. Your words cannot be taken back once they are released from your mouth. Take a moment, take a day, take however long you need to not disrespect someone else. Let them be the one to apologize to you for their actions not vice versa. No one deserves the satisfaction of you losing your dignity. You are better than that! You are.

When you understand your worth… You are worthy of love. You are worthy of real friendships of equal value. You deserve everything this life has to offer you. Do you realize this? Do not allow anyone to mistreat, disrespect, abuse you; mentally, emotionally, physically, or make you feel less than.

Do you consider yourself worthy? Why are you worthy of respect? Do you respect others? What changes are necessary to ensure others value you?

Use the following journal page to write your thoughts.

Journal Page

15

Don't Speak

Don't speak! Often, many people will interject themselves into places, conversations, situations that they were never invited into in the first place. If I didn't ask, it is because I did not want to know or cannot handle the response you may provide. Please learn to stop volunteering unsolicited advice and conversations to others and then getting upset because they are uninterested or did not respond the way you feel they should have.

It is all about improving your lifestyle and that means everything that encompasses it. Everything! Adults communicate. Adults disagree. Adults can agree to disagree because not always will you see eye to eye. I can appreciate someone having a difference of opinion but at least attempt to hear me, not just listen.

Men lie. Women lie. But why? A lot of hurt feelings can be avoided if people were more honest with themselves and others. Simple things I have found people will be dishonest about. People lose respect for someone that is dishonest. Are you a man or woman of integrity? If so, you cannot be a person of integrity and a liar too. It is a total contradiction.

Just as God affords us grace, I feel we should be willing to extend grace to others as well. But we should not take God's grace for granted or anyone else's for that matter. Don't speak the first thing that comes to mind when dealing with others. Take your time to think about what you will say because you cannot gauge how the other person will receive your message. Don't speak just to hear yourself talking. Speak to bring about something positive.

What could you identify about yourself in this chapter? Do you bend the truth a little too often? Do you extend grace to others? Do you contradict yourself often? Do you interject yourself a lot unto others?

Use the following journal page to write your thoughts.

Journal Page

16

Open Invitation

"Hurry, hurry… step right on in!" You extend an open invitation to everything you allow to enter your lifestyle. This includes your mind, body, and spirit. Although, I have never been big on dieting I know there are others who take this extremely seriously. The fact is, I know my body.

What I will say, you are what you eat. It will show up in every aspect of your life at some point and you need to be fully aware of this. Consult a doctor, a nutritionist, whomever you need to consult to get to a healthier you. I will not lie to myself and say I will diet, but I can cut back on my weaknesses. I can also incorporate exercise more frequently into my weekly routine.

This invitation also applies to explorations. What are you doing new and exciting? Are you stepping outside of your comfort zones? You do not need to break the bank to open yourself up to trying new experiences, new adventures. When was the last time you got in your car and drove to the beach or to the mountains? When was the last time you drove to your happy place?

Unfortunately, at this time we are experiencing restrictions like we have never seen in our lifetime. However, this will not last always so plan what you would like to do first when this is over. Introduce your children and grandchildren to things that you may not have experienced. Schedule date nights with your spouse or friends.

This new year promise yourself that you will live a little and that you are going to be open to creating a new lifestyle, the lifestyle that you have always imagined for yourself. Now it no longer has to be a dream because you will begin taking steps no matter how small to make efforts to make it happen! Do not fear what anyone else has to say or what they will say. After all, this is your life to live - it was given to you. If you can live with your choices and sleep well at night, I say go for it. I always encourage others to be responsible and remember there are always consequences to our actions. Always. What is done in the dark always surfaces into the light, make no mistake about it. Can you handle it? That is one of the precautions I will say take when creating this lifestyle. Make sure you can live with any decision made.

Be bold. Do not live-in fear. Is there someone that you long to tell how you feel about them? Is there someone that you want to make peace with? Extend an open invitation to resolve the conflict. Be intentional in your actions. Whatever you decide to do in your pursuit to a lifestyle you can be proud to call your own, make sure it is with real intentions to make a change for the betterment of you and the way you view and live your life going forward.

"I hope you dance." I hope we all can have a good "dance as if no one is watching" in our lives more than once. I hope we can laugh uncontrollably even at ourselves at times. I hope we stop to smell the flowers. I hope we place our feet on solid ground and leave footprints in the sand. I hope we know what it is like to experience a moment of meditation in our lives throughout the day, to take a reset or a pause.

I hope we are able to taste our favorite dish at least once a month. Perhaps, with our favorite glass of wine or music. Are you getting any of this? I hope you live and love. I hope you do things that bring you immeasurable joy and happiness in this lifetime. I hope you live with no regrets. I hope you dream. I hope you dance in the rain. I hope you live with no regrets. I hope you dream. I hope you dance in the rain. I hope you run as fast as you can. I hope you live beautiful one. LIVE. This is your open invitation to live a beautiful life. Conquer your fears and erase all doubts.

Invite an intimate relationship with God like you have never experienced before. Make an intentional effort to commit to devoting quality time understanding your spirit man. Increase your prayer life and meditation. Invite a new you to be born in this lifestyle that you create for yourself. It begins now…

What will you do with this open invitation to live differently? How will you begin? What do you fear if anything of doing but have always wanted to do? Will you make that call or write that letter to that someone you know that you should? What was your greatest takeaway from this chapter? Are you committed to creating a lifestyle for you and your family that you can be proud to call your own?

Use the following journal page to write your thoughts.

Journal Page

17

Shine Bright

"Do not dull your shine for anyone." That is right - anyone! You have worked hard to get to where you are right now in life. Extremely hard. You did the work! At times, you wondered if you would make it through. Faith is what kept you. Faith keeps you even now! You have left behaviors and habits behind and you are looking forward to a brighter future. You have set goals for yourself and one by one you are crossing them off.

You are proud of yourself. I am proud of you. Do you know why I am proud of you? Because I am you, you are me. We all have overcome so much in life. If we only search for the good instead of the bad in others and recognize that we have so much more in common than we realize, we could work together for better days. I want to see you excel. You should also want me to excel. Why would you ever want to see someone down? Examine your heart.

Your shine should not come from the exterior. Your shine should always come from within. Your inner glow is what should exude outwardly. Working on your spirituality; building a closer relationship with God.

There is not a day that goes by that you should not utter the words "thank you!"

"Thank you, Lord, for another day."

"Thank you for life, health and strength."

"Thank you for my family."

"Thank you for being my provider."

You get the point…. There is so much to be thankful for. You should never be at a loss for words in your thanksgiving each day. Every single day. I am grateful, humbled, and forever thankful for every blessing.

The fact that I have overcome things meant to destroy me and can still smile is a testament within itself. Many times, we do not want to think about or relive difficult memories but instead view it has a celebration. You made it through. You went through the fire. You are shining bright. Keep going. Keep building the lifestyle that you dream of. It is possible.

There is nothing impossible.
I can do all things through Christ who strengthens me"
Philippians 4:13

Remember this…
Always!!!

What is your takeaway? What do you feel was most beneficial to you in this read? Was it the thought provoking questions at the end of each chapter? Which chapter has you wanting to go back and read again?

Use the following journal page to write your thoughts.

Journal Page

18

Sharing Is Caring

What are your pearls of wisdom that you feel others can benefit from regarding your perceptions, lifestyles, things to help grow yourself for the betterment of you?

Use the following journal section below to share your thoughts.

Journal Section

_____
_____
_____
_____
_____
_____
_____
_____
_____
_____
_____
_____
_____
_____
_____

CLOSING THOUGHTS

Thank you for investing in my endeavors to help others become better versions of themselves from my books (leandrearivers.com) to my home and fashion collections (Shoplaowens.com).

It is my passion to see others living life to the fullest. As an author I continue to fulfill my dreams through my books which are a necessary tool which embodies my mentorship, motivation, inspiration as my stories spread worldwide in efforts to heal and restore.

Every day we are alive I honestly believe is another opportunity for us to make a difference in someone else's life. It is my prayer that you will sincerely think about every chapter read and implement the positives to your own life and share with those you feel can benefit from it as well. My instinct is to look for solutions first when faced with life's challenges. Let us not become a part of this world's problems, but instead be the difference that this world is in dire need of.

Shop L.A. Owens is my online boutique where you can shop some of my favorite must-haves for your home. You will find much of what I enjoy daily in my own home. If you are seeking some direction in creating a new wardrobe or some image inspiration, I am sure you will be well pleased with the many shop the look collections. Remember to create a lifestyle you can be proud to call your own.

Leandrea Rivers

www.ingramcontent.com/pod-product-compliance
Lightning Source LLC
Chambersburg PA
CBHW071155090426
42736CB00012B/2344